Puffin Books

The Puffin Book of Funny Verse

Some of the best-loved poems in the English language were written to raise a laugh: T. S. Eliot's cat poems, A. A. Milne's 'Buckingham Palace' and Edward Lear's 'The Jumblies' are all clever and serious and *funny*. It's a tradition that the poets of today continue – Spike Milligan, of course:

> Today I saw a little worm
> Wriggling on his belly.
> Perhaps he'd like to come inside
> And see what's on the Telly.

But also Ted Hughes and Russell Hoban, Charles Causley and George Barker. And Michael Rosen:

> Ask no questions
> tell no lies.
> Ever seen mincemeat
> in mince pies?

In this book are collected some of the funniest poems, old and new, ever written. And since many of the poets (Belloc, Lear, Milligan) could also draw, we have included their own pictures wherever possible.

If you like poetry, but most of all if you like laughing, this is the book for you – no matter what your age.

The Puffin Book of Funny Verse

Compiled by Julia Watson

PUFFIN BOOKS

in association with

FABER AND FABER

PUFFIN BOOKS

Published by the Penguin Group
27 Wrights Lane, London W8 5TZ, England
Viking Penguin Inc., 40 West 23rd Street, New York, New York 10010, USA
Penguin Books Australia Ltd, Ringwood, Victoria, Australia
Penguin Books Canada Ltd, 2801 John Street, Markham, Ontario, Canada L3R 1B4
Penguin Books (NZ) Ltd, 182–190 Wairau Road, Auckland 10, New Zealand

Penguin Books Ltd, Registered Offices: Harmondsworth, Middlesex, England

This collection first published by Faber and Faber 1979 in association with
Guild Publishing, a division of Book Club Associates
Published in Puffin Books 1981
9 10

The original illustrations accompany the poems on the following
pages: 8, 9, 18/19, 24, 29, 44, 56, 62, 64, 84, 85, 88/89,
97, 100, 104/105, 110/111, 124,
Additional material is by; Peter Clarke, 20/21, 28, 31, 32/33, 37, 40,
55, 70/71, 74, 75, 82, 94/95, 106/107, 108, 119, 127;
Frances Livens, 10, 11, 15, 23, 26/27, 43, 48, 53, 60, 61, 69, 78, 79,
86/87, 98, 113, 115, 120/121;
Donald Rooum, 12/13, 17, 46, 47, 50, 58, 59, 66, 67, 72, 73, 76/77,
80/81, 90/91, 117, 123.

Printed and bound in Great Britain by
Cox & Wyman Ltd, Reading
Set in Baskerville

Contents

Unusual Animals & Crazy Creatures

Odd Bods & Funny Folk

Rhymes, Riddles, Logic & Folly

Treks & Travels

Adventures & Mishaps

Unusual Animals & Crazy Creatures

The Bison
Hilaire Belloc

The Bison is vain, and (I write it with pain)
The Door-mat you see on his head
Is not, as some learned professors maintain,
The opulent growth of a genius' brain;
But is sewn on with needle and thread.

Howard

A. A. Milne

There was a young puppy called Howard,
Who at fighting was rather a coward;
He never quite ran
When the battle began,
But he started at once to bow-wow hard.

The Kangaroo
Anonymous

Old Jumpety-Bumpety-Hop-and-Go-One
Was lying asleep on his side in the sun.
This old kangaroo, he was whisking the flies
(With his long glossy tail) from his ears and his eyes.
Jumpety-Bumpety-Hop-and-Go-One
Was lying asleep on his side in the sun,
Jumpety-Bumpety-Hop!

Jump or Jiggle
Evelyn Beyer

Frogs jump
Caterpillars hump

Worms wiggle
Bugs jiggle

Rabbits lop
Horses clop

Snakes slide
Sea-gulls glide

Mice creep
Deer leap

Puppies bounce
Kittens pounce

Lions stalk –
But –
I *walk*!

The Swank
V. C. Vickers

The Swank is quick and full of vice,
He tortures beetles also mice.
He bites their legs off and he beats them
Into a pulp, and then he eats them.

Silly Old Baboon
Spike Milligan

There was a Baboon
Who, one afternoon,
Said, 'I think I will fly to the sun.'
So, with two great palms
Strapped to his arms,
He started his take-off run.

Mile after mile
He galloped in style
But never once left the ground.
'You're running too slow,'
Said a passing crow,
'Try reaching the speed of sound.'

So he put on a spurt –
By God how it hurt!
The soles of his feet caught fire.
There were great clouds of steam
As he raced through a stream
But he still didn't get any higher.

Racing on through the night,
Both his knees caught alight
And smoke billowed out from his rear.
Quick to his aid
Came a fire brigade
Who chased him for over a year.

Many moons passed by.
Did Baboon ever fly?
Did he ever get to the sun?
I've just heard today
That he's well on his way!
He'll be passing through Acton at one.

P.S. Well, what do you expect from a Baboon?

The Angry Hens from Never-when
Michael Rosen

The angry hens from Never-when
had a fight and lost their legs.
Now it's hot
where they squat
and they're laying soft-boiled eggs.

The Purple Cow
Gelett Burgess

Reflections on a Mythic Beast,
Who's Quite Remarkable at Least.

I never saw a Purple Cow,
I never hope to see one:
But I can tell you, anyhow,
I'd rather see than be one.

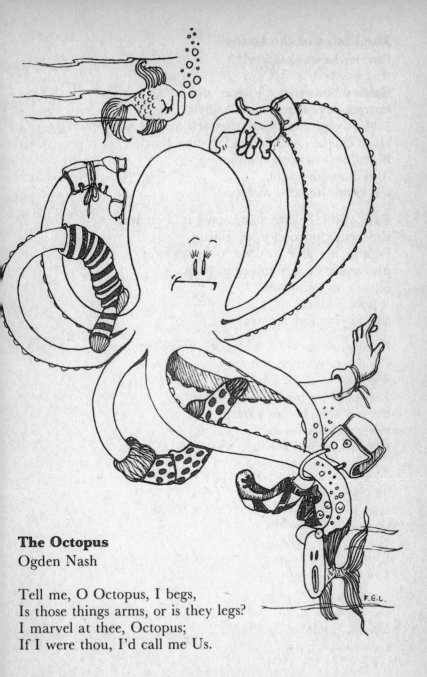

The Octopus
Ogden Nash

Tell me, O Octopus, I begs,
Is those things arms, or is they legs?
I marvel at thee, Octopus;
If I were thou, I'd call me Us.

15

The Plaint of the Camel

Charles Edward Carryl

Canary-birds feed on sugar and seed,
Parrots have crackers to crunch;
And as for the poodles, they tell me the noodles
Have chicken and cream for their lunch.
But there's never a question
About MY digestion,
ANYTHING does for me.

Cats, you're aware, can repose in a chair,
Chickens can roost upon rails;
Puppies are able to sleep in a stable,
And oysters can slumber in pails.
But no one supposes
A poor Camel dozes.
ANY PLACE does for me.

Lambs are enclosed where it's never exposed,
Coops are constructed for hens;
Kittens are treated to houses well heated,
And pigs are protected by pens.
But a Camel comes handy
Wherever it's sandy,
ANYWHERE does for me.

People would laugh if you rode a giraffe,
Or mounted the back of an ox;
It's nobody's habit to ride on a rabbit,
Or try to bestraddle a fox.
But as for a Camel, he's
Ridden by families –
ANY LOAD does for me.

A snake is as round as a hole in the ground;
Weasels are wavy and sleek;
And no alligator could ever be straighter
Than lizards that live in a creek.
But a Camel's all lumpy,
And bumpy, and humpy,
ANY SHAPE does for me.

The Elephant
Hilaire Belloc

When people bear this beast to mind,
They marvel more and more
At such a LITTLE tail behind,
So LARGE a trunk before.

 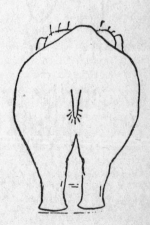

The Old Gumbie Cat T. S. Eliot

I have a Gumbie Cat in mind, her name is Jennyanydots;
Her coat is of the tabby kind, with tiger stripes and leopard spots.
All day she sits upon the stair or on the steps or on the mat:
She sits and sits and sits and sits – and that's what makes a Gumbie Cat!
But when the day's hustle and bustle is done,
Then the Gumbie Cat's work is but hardly begun.
And when all the family's in bed and asleep,
She tucks up her skirts to the basement to creep.
She is deeply concerned with the ways of the mice –
Their behaviour's not good and their manners not nice;
So when she has got them lined up on the matting,
She teaches them music, crocheting and tatting.

I have a Gumbie Cat in mind, her name is Jennyanydots;
Her equal would be hard to find, she likes the warm and sunny spots.
All day she sits beside the hearth or on the bed or on my hat:
She sits and sits and sits and sits – and that's what makes a Gumbie Cat!
But when the day's hustle and bustle is done,
Then the Gumbie Cat's work is but hardly begun.
As she finds that the mice will not ever keep quiet,
She is sure it is due to irregular diet;
And believing that nothing is done without trying,
She sets right to work with her baking and frying.
She makes them a mouse-cake of bread and dried peas,
And a *beautiful* fry of lean bacon and cheese.

I have a Gumbie Cat in mind, her name is Jennyanydots;
The curtain-cord she likes to wind, and tie it into sailor-knots.
She sits upon the window-sill, or anything that's smooth and flat:
She sits and sits and sits and sits – and that's what makes a Gumbie Cat!
But when the day's hustle and bustle is done,
Then the Gumbie Cat's work is but hardly begun.
She thinks that the cockroaches just need employment
To prevent them from idle and wanton destroyment.
So she's formed, from that lot of disorderly louts,
A troop of well-disciplined helpful boy-scouts,
With a purpose in life and a good deed to do –
And she's even created a Beetles' Tattoo.

So for Old Gumbie Cats let us now give three cheers –
On whom well-ordered households depend, it appears.

The Common Cormorant

Anonymous

The common cormorant or shag
Lays eggs inside a paper bag
The reason you will see no doubt
It is to keep the lightning out.
But what these unobservant birds
Have never noticed is that herds
Of wandering bears may come with buns
And steal the bags to hold the crumbs.

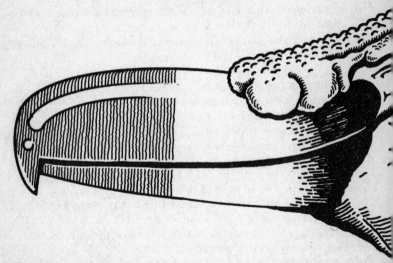

The Moon Bird

V. C. Vickers

These birds frequent the rolling plains,
(The eggs are puce with purple stains)
They live in herds
These curious birds,
And feed on rubbish and remains.

The Vulture
Hilaire Belloc

The vulture eats between his meals,
And that's the reason why
He very, very rarely feels
As well as you or I.

His eye is dull, his head is bald,
His neck is growing thinner.
Oh! What a lesson for us all
To only eat at dinner!

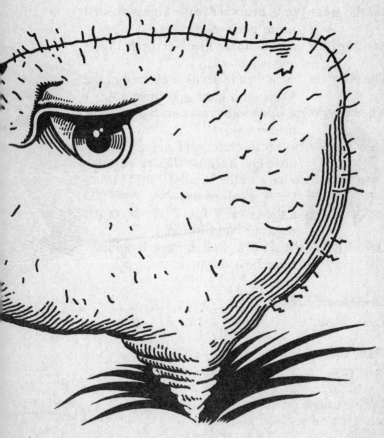

Among the Mountains of Spitzbergen roam the ghosts of the great Bears

George Barker

Among the Mountains of Spitzbergen roam the
     ghosts of great Bears
And on his back each one a coat worth an entire
     fortune wears.
The Hunters from such shops as Harrods or the
     Bradley Fur Trading Co:
Armed with howitzers and hatchets hunt them
     down across the snow.
But the great White Bears are really ghosts dressed
     up in garbs of fur
And they flit among the ice like Northern Lights
     only silenter.
The Hunters, being simple, think they've shot the
     bears with guns and bows
When they come upon some fur coats lying empty
     in the snows.
They pack them up in crates and parcels,
          furtively, because they're cowards.
Then ship them back to the Bradley Fur Trading
     Co & to Harrods.
But the ghosts of the Great White Polar Bears are
     dancing hand in hand
Round the North Pole at Spitzbergen laughing
     fit to beat the band.

The Polar Bear
Hilaire Belloc

The Polar Bear is unaware
Of cold that cuts me through:
For why? He has a coat of hair.
I wish I had one too!

I'm not frightened of Pussy Cats
Spike Milligan

I'm not frightened of Pussy Cats,
They only eat up mice and rats,
But a Hippopotamus
Could eat the Lotofus!

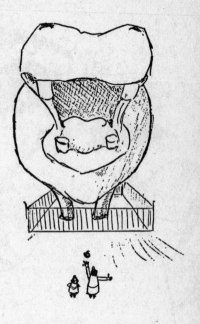

My Dog
Anonymous

I've got a dog as thin as a rail,
He's got fleas all over his tail;
Every time his tail goes flop,
The fleas on the bottom all hop to the top.

The Yellow Cat
Gregory Harrison

'There he is,' yells Father,
Grabbing lumps of soil,
'That yellow tabby's on the fence.
Drown him in boiling oil.
He's scratching at my runner beans.
Bang at the window, quick.
Wait till I get my laces done
I'll beat him with my stick.'

'Too late,' they shout, 'he's on the fence.
He's turning, Father, wait.'

'I'll give him turning, I'll be there,
I'll serve him on a plate.'

They banged the window, Father stormed
And hopped with wild despair;
The cat grew fat with insolence
And froze into a stare.
Its brazen glare stopped Father
With its blazing yellow light;
The silken shape turned slowly
And dropped gently out of sight.

One Day at a Perranporth Pet-Shop

Charles Causley

One day at a Perranporth pet-shop
On a rather wild morning in June,
A lady from Par bought a Budgerigar
And she sang to a curious tune:
'Say that you love me, my sweetheart,
My darling, my dovey, my pride,
My very own jewel, my dear one!'
'Oh, lumme', the budgie replied.

'I'll feed you entirely on cream-cakes
And doughnuts all smothered in jam,
And puddings and pies of incredible size,
And peaches and melons and ham.
And you shall drink whiskies and sodas,
For comfort your cage shall be famed.
You shall sleep in a bed lined with satin.'
'Oh, crikey!' the budgie exclaimed.

But the lady appeared not to hear him
For she showed neither sorrow nor rage,
As with common-sense tardy and action foolhardy
She opened the door of his cage.
'Come perch on my finger, my honey,
To show you are mine, O my sweet!' –
Whereupon the poor fowl with a shriek and a howl
Took off like a jet down the street.

And high he flew up above Cornwall
To ensure his escape was no failure,
Then his speed he increased and flew south and east
To his ancestral home in Australia.
For although to the Australian abo
The word 'budgerigar' means 'good food',
He said, 'I declare I'll feel much safer there
Than in Bodmin or Bugle or Bude.'

MORAL

And I'm sure with the budgie's conclusion
You all will agree without fail:
Best eat frugal and free in a far-distant tree
Than down all the wrong diet in jail.

Bees
Russell Hoban

Honeybees are very tricky –
Honey doesn't make them sticky.

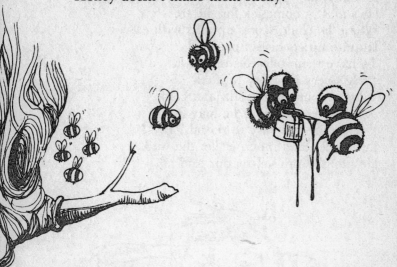

The Firefly
Ogden Nash

The firefly's flame
Is something for which science has no name.
I can think of nothing eerier
Than flying around with an unidentified glow on
                    a person's posterior.

Armadillo

Mary Innes

An Armadillo as a pet
Is something you won't soon forget.
He's mostly homesick for the trees
Where he could scoop up ants with ease.
It quite upsets his simple soul
To have them offered in a bowl.
   He's very little joy to hold,
   In armour-plating stiff and cold.
   Whate'er affections he may feel,
   They are not easy to reveal,
But stuffed and mounted on the wall,
He's loudly praised by one and all.

Today I saw a little worm
Spike Milligan

Today I saw a little worm
Wriggling on his belly.
Perhaps he'd like to come inside
And see what's on the Telly.

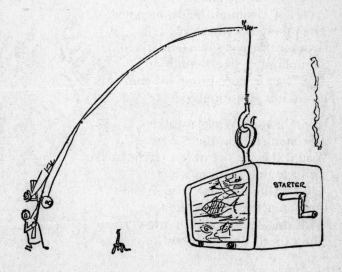

The Kwackagee

James Reeves

Back in the bleak and blurry days
When all was murk and mystery –
That is (if I may mint a phrase)
Before the dawn of history.
Professors think there used to be,
Not far from Waikee-waike,
A monster called the Kwackagee,
A sort of flying snake.

This animile, they all agree,
Was forty feet in length,
Would spiral up the tallest tree
And then with all his strength
Propel himself with sinuous grace
And undulation muscular
To find another feeding-place
In some far vale crepuscular.

Expert opinions are two
About his mode of travel;
Professor Grommit holds one view;
The other, Doctor Gravvle.
Grommit believes he could give off
Some kind of speed-emulsion;
The Doctor, ever prone to scoff,
Postulates jet-propulsion.

In prehistoric Waikee-waike,
The men (if men there were),
Would they in breathless terror quake
To hear that rattling whirr
As flew the monster through the sky?
Or would they brave the foe
With missile and with battle-cry?
The experts do not know.

The Whale
Theodore Roethke

There was a most Monstrous Whale:
He had no Skin, he had no Tail.
When he tried to Spout, that Great Big Lubber,
The best he could do was Jiggle his Blubber.

Yak

William Jay Smith

The long-haired Yak has long black hair.
He lets it grow – he doesn't care.
He lets it grow and grow and grow,
He lets it trail along the stair.
Does he ever go to the barbershop? NO!
How wild and woolly and devil-may-care
A long-haired Yak with long black hair
Would look when perched in a barber chair!

Pigs
Jack Prelutsky

Pigs are stout
and pigs are kind
and pigs are seldom clean.

snout before
and tail behind
and bacon in between

The Geese in Greece
N. M. Bodecker

The geese
in Greece
grow white
woolly fleece,
which is made
into shawls
in the Peloponnese.
Nice
heartwarming
geese.

Odd Bods & Funny Folk

Mister Beers
Hugh Lofting

This is Mister Beers;
And for forty-seven years
He's been digging in his garden like a miner.
He isn't planting seeds
Nor scratching up the weeds,
He's trying to bore a tunnel down to China.

Go North, South, East and West, Young Man
Spike Milligan

Drake is going West, lads,
So Tom is going East;
But tiny Fred
Just lies in bed,
The lazy little beast.

Edward the Confessor
E. Clerihew Bentley

Edward the Confessor
Slept under the dresser.
When that began to pall,
He slept in the hall.

Piano Practice

Ian Serraillier

A doting father once there was
Who loved his daughter Gerda,
Until she got the piano craze –
Then how the passion stirred her!
Her fingers were wild elephants' feet,
And as month after month he heard her.
He tried every way
To stop her play
From bribery to murder.

One day when she was practising,
He popped up behind and caught her
And dumped her in his wheelbarrow
And carried her off to slaughter.

Tipping her into a well, he cried,
'Hurrah! I've drowned my daughter!'
But a voice from the well
Rang out like a bell,
'Aha – there isn't any water!'

Stately Verse

Anonymous

If Mary goes far out to sea,
By wayward breezes fanned,
I'd like to know – can you tell me?–
Just where would Maryland?

If Tenny went high up in air
And looked o'er land and lea,
Looked here and there and everywhere,
Pray what would Tennessee?

I looked out of the window and
Saw Orry on the lawn;
He's not there now, and who can tell
Just where has Oregon?

Two girls were quarrelling one day
With garden tools, and so
I said, 'My dears, let Mary rake
And just let Idaho.'

A friend of mine lived in a flat
With half a dozen boys;
When he fell ill I asked him why.
He said: 'I'm Illinois.'

An English lady had a steed.
She called him 'Ighland Bay.
She rode for exercise, and thus
Rhode Island every day.

My Sister Clarissa spits twice if I kiss her

George Barker

My sister Clarissa spits twice if I kiss her
and once if I hold her hand.
I reprimand her – my name's Alexander –
for spitting I simply can't stand.

'Clarissa, Clarissa, my sister, is this a
really nice habit to practise?'
But she always replies with innocent eyes
rather softly, 'Dear Brother, the fact is

I think I'm an ape with a very small grape
crushed to juice in my mastodon lips.
Since I am not a prude, though I hate being rude,
I am simply ejecting the pips.'

King Foo Foo

Charles Causley

King Foo Foo sat upon his throne
Dressed in his royal closes,
While all round his courtiers stood
With clothes-pegs on their noses.

'This action strange,' King Foo Foo said,
'My mind quite discomposes,
Though vulgar curiosity
A good king never shoses.'

But to the court it was as clear
As poetry or prose is:
King Foo Foo had not had a bath
Since goodness only knoses.

But one fine day the Fire Brigade
Rehearsing with their hoses
(To Handel's 'Water Music' played
With many puffs and bloses)

Quite failed the water to control
In all its ebbs and floses
And simply drenched the king with sev-
Eral thousand gallon doses.

At this each knight (though impolite)
A mighty grin exposes.
'At last,' the King said, 'now I see
That all my court morose is!

'A debt to keep his courtiers gay
A monarch surely owses,
And deep within my royal breast
A sporting heart reposes.'

So now each night its water bright
The Fire Brigade disposes
Over a King who smells as sweet
As all the royal roses.

Contrary Mary
Nancy Byrd Turner

You ask why Mary was called contrary?
Well, this is why, my dear:
She planted the most outlandish things
In her garden every year:
She was always sowing the queerest seed,
And when advised to stop,
Her answer was merely, 'No, indeed –
Just wait till you see the crop!'

And here are some of the crops, my child
(Although not nearly all):
Bananarcissus and cucumberries,
And violettuce small;
Potatomatoes, melonions rare,
And rhubarberries round,
With porcupineapples prickly-rough
On a little bush close to the ground.

She gathered the stuff in mid-July
And sent it away to sell –
And now you'll see how she earned her name,
And how she earned it well.
Were the crops hauled off in a farmer's cart?
No, not by any means,
But in little June-buggies and automobeetles
And dragonflying machines!

The Daughter of the Farrier
Anonymous

The daughter of the farrier
Could find no one to marry her,
Because she said
She would not wed
A man who could not carry her.

The foolish girl was wrong enough,
And had to wait quite long enough;
For as she sat
She grew so fat
That nobody was strong enough.

Uncle

Harry Graham

Uncle, whose inventive brains
Kept evolving aeroplanes,
Fell from an enormous height
On my garden lawn, last night.
Flying is a fatal sport,
Uncle wrecked the tennis-court.

Miss Torrent
Gregory Harrison

Little Miss Torrent drives a car.
Nothing surprising in that?
You'd think there was if you saw her ride by
Resplendent in flowery hat;
For little Miss Torrent,
Hunched over the wheel,
Scares everybody in town;
When people see her rushing along
They're sure she will batter them down.
They squirm as she crashes the gears and screams
With a stab of the brake to a stop;
They cover their faces to shut out the sight
As she spins on the ice like a top.
They daren't use the crossing
For fear she is blind
To the lollipop man with his stick;
As she squeezes the kerb with a squeal of her tyres
Pedestrians feel dizzy and sick.
But when you are driving yourself it is worst
For she scorches the old village street
As if she were driving a rallying car
With a champion racer to beat.
And by far worst of all are the deep narrow lanes
If you happen to see her approach,
For the lane is suddenly as dangerous as if
You were meeting a six-wheeler coach;
For she rarely pays heed to the motorist's code
And invariably drives the wrong side of the road.

A Merry Game
Carolyn Wells

Betty and Belinda Ames
Had the pleasantest of games;
'Twas to hid from one another
Marmaduke, their baby brother.
Once Belinda, little love,
Hid the baby in the stove;
Such a joke! for little Bet
Hasn't found the baby yet.

Sneaky Bill
William Cole

I'm Sneaky Bill, I'm terrible mean and vicious,
I steal all the cashews
   from the mixed-nuts dishes;
I eat all the icing but I won't touch the cake,
And what you won't give me,
I'll go ahead and take.

I gobble the cherries from everyone's drinks,
And whenever there are sausages
I grab a dozen links;
  I take both drumsticks if
  there's turkey or chicken,
  And the biggest strawberries
  are what I'm pickin';

I make sure I get the finest chop on the plate,
And I'll eat the portions of anyone who's late!

I'm always on the spot before the dinner bell –
I guess I'm pretty awful,
        But
         I
           do
             eat
               well!

Politeness

Harry Graham

My cousin John was most polite;
He led shortsighted Mrs Bond,
By accident, one winter's night
Into a village pond.
Her life perhaps he might have saved
But how genteelly he behaved!

Each time she rose and waved to him
He smiled and bowed and doffed his hat;
Thought he, although I cannot swim,
At least I can do that –
And when for the third time she sank
He stood bareheaded on the bank.

Be civil, then, to young and old;
Especially to persons who
Possess a quantity of gold
Which they might leave to you.
The more they have, it seems to me,
The more polite you ought to be.

Good and Bad Children

Robert Louis Stevenson

Children, you are very little,
And your bones are very brittle;
If you would grow great and stately,
You must try to walk sedately.

You must still be bright and quiet,
And content with simple diet;
And remain, through all bewild'ring,
Innocent and honest children.

Happy hearts and happy faces,
Happy play in grassy places –
That was how, in ancient ages,
Children grew to kings and sages.

But the unkind and the unruly,
And the sort who eat unduly,
They must never hope for glory –
Theirs is quite a different story!

Cruel children, crying babies,
All grow up as geese and gabies,
Hated, as their age increases,
By their nephews and their nieces.

Old Mr Bows
Wilma Horsbrugh

I'm old Mr Bows
Whom nobody knows
And my beard is so long that it tickles my toes,
In the front door I shut it.
While I 'Tut-tut-tutted'
My wife took a knife and helpfully cut it.

Now I'm old Mr Bows
With a cold id by dose
And I'll never get warm till my beard again
                                          grows.

Atishoo!

My Uncle Dan

Ted Hughes

My Uncle Dan's an inventor, you may think that's
                very fine.
You may wish he was your Uncle instead of being mine –
If he wanted he could make a watch that bounces
                when it drops,
He could make a helicopter out of string and bottle tops
Or any really useful thing you can't get in the shops.
But Uncle Dan has other ideas:
The bottomless glass for ginger beers,
The toothless saw that's safe for the tree,
A special word for a spelling bee
(Like Lionocerangoutangadder),
Or the roll-uppable rubber ladder,
The mystery pie that bites when it's bit –
My Uncle Dan invented it.
My Uncle Dan sits in his den inventing night and day.
His eyes peer from his hair and beard like mice
                from a load of hay.
And does he make the shoes that will go walks
                without your feet?
A shrinker to shrink instantly the elephants you meet?
A carver that just carves from the air steaks
                cooked and ready to eat?
No, no, he has other intentions –
Only perfectly useless inventions:
Glassless windows (they never break),
A medicine to cure the earthquake,
The unspillable screwed-down cup,
The stairs that go neither down nor up,
The door you simply paint on a wall –
Uncle Dan invented them all.

Stables' Tables
Roy Fuller

There was a girl called Sheila Stables
Who never really knew her tables.
At least, with study she was able
To get to know the twice times table;
Then having had revealed the trick,
She learned her ten times fairly quick.
A friend of hers called Mabel Gimpel
Said five and eleven were just as simple,
But Sheila never found this so.
Particularly hard to know
Were nine and seven times. Miss Bass
(Who took the mathematics class)
Would call out: 'Sheila Stables, what
Are seven nines? ... Oh no, they're not.'

Her bad marks in this subject rather
Worried her. She told her father,
Who laughed and said: 'Why goodness me,
There are more vital matters, She,
Than learning boring things by heart –
For instance, human love, and art.'
A poetic man was Mr Stables
Who'd never quite got right *his* tables
And if required to do a sum
Would use four fingers and a thumb.

'What's nine times seven?' asked Miss Bass.
'Only, my father says, an ass
Would know the answer,' Sheila said,
Though not without a sense of dread.
'I asked you, not your father,' Miss
Bass cried. 'Nought out of ten for this.'

Whether in later life Sheila Stables
Had ever mastered all her tables
I do not know, but she became
A greater player of the game
Than even the formidable Bass.
She worked out when the sun would pass
Behind the planet Minotaur
(A body quite unknown before
The book of astronomic tables
Compiled by Dr Sheila Stables);
And put, the right way up, a bit
Of puzzle Einstein failed to fit.

It seemed the word did not depend
On having at one's fingers' end
Nine eights or seven sixes – though
Poetry itself could never show
(As Sheila was the first to say)
The Past, the Purpose and the Way:
Somewhere among the curious laws
Enacted by the Primal Cause
There enters (usually in the heavens)
Such things as nine, or seven, sevens.

A Fat Old Farmer

Gregory Harrison

A fat old farmer in the wolds
Was always catching dreadful colds;
He wrapped a stocking round his throat
And always wore an extra coat.
He sneezed and sneezed until his wife
Feared he would sneeze away his life.

She called to the hen-yard, 'Come, get into bed!'
He sneezed a great hole in the side of the shed.
She hurried downstairs and said, 'Lean on my
                                            arm.'
And he gave a great sneeze that shook the whole
                                            farm.
'Come,get in the wagon. To the hospital, quick!'
And the hay filled the lane from a sneeze-flattened
                                            rick.
The horse turned its head, took one look at the
                                            face,
And tore down the lane at a furious pace.

So they sent for the doctor who said, 'He is ill.'
And he chose a bright scarlet, rectangular pill.
They laid him down gently and prepared to
                                            retreat,
And they opened his mouth and anchored his feet.
'Push it down,' yelled the doctor and the red pill
                                            got stuck.
The farmer got angry and quacked like a duck.
The pain was so sharp that he missed the next
                                            sneeze;
He shook off the doctor and crawled to his knees.
'I've got a sore throat. That pill's like a brick.'
'Yes,' the doctor agreed, 'it's my favourite trick.'

The Gentle Governor
Irene Gough

The Governor, the Governor,
Said: 'Let there be no flurry,
I only fall off camels
When I am in a hurry;
I reach the ground
Without a sound,
There is no need for worry.'

Inconsiderate Hannah

Harry Graham

Naughty little Hannah said
She could make her Grandma whistle,
So, that night, inside her bed,
Placed some nettles and a thistle.

Though dear Grandma quite infirm is,
Heartless Hannah watched her settle,
With her poor old epidermis
Resting up against a nettle.

Suddenly she reached the thistle!
My! you should have heard her whistle.

* * * * * * * *

A successful plan was Hannah's
But I cannot praise her manners.

Godfrey Gordon Gustavus Gore

William Brighty Rands

Godfrey Gordon Gustavus Gore –
No doubt you have heard the name before –
Was a boy who never would shut a door!

The wind might whistle, the wind might roar,
And teeth be aching and throats be sore,
But still he never would shut the door.

His father would beg, his mother implore,
'Godfrey Gordon Gustavus Gore,
We really *do* wish you would shut the door!'

Their hands they wrung, their hair they tore;
But Godfrey Gordon Gustavus Gore
Was deaf as the buoy out at the Nore.

When he walked forth the folks would roar,
'Godfrey Gordon Gustavus Gore
Why don't you think to shut the door?'

They rigged out a Shutter with sail and oar,
And threatened to pack off Gustavus Gore
On a voyage of penance to Singapore.

But he begged for mercy, and said, 'No more!
Pray do not send me to Singapore
On a Shutter, and then I will shut the door!'

'You will?' said his parents; 'then keep on shore!
But mind you do! For the plague is sore
Of a fellow that never will shut the door,
Godfrey Gordon Gustavus Gore!'

How Sad

William Cole

There's a pitiful story – ah, me!
Of a young English girl named Nellie,
Who stared dumbly all day at TV
(Which in England is known as 'the telly') –
She died ... and the reason, you see,
Was her brains had all turned into jelly!

Kings
Walter de la Mare

King Canute
Sat down by the sea,
Up washed the tide
And away went he.

Good King Alfred
Cried, 'My sakes!
Not five winks,
And look at those cakes!'

Lackland John
Were a right royal Tartar
Till he made his mark
Upon *Magna Carta*:

Ink, seal, table,
On Runnymede green,
Anno Domini
12 – 15.

Deborah Delora

Anonymous

Deborah Delora, she liked a bit of fun –
She went to the baker's and she bought a penny bun,
Dipped the bun in treacle and threw it at her teacher –
Deborah Delora! What a wicked creature!

Lazy Lucy

N. M. Bodecker

Lazy Lucy
lay in bed.
Lazy Lucy's
mother said:
'You will drive
your mother crazy.
Upsy-daisy,
Lucy Lazy!'
To her mom
said Lazy Lucy,
'Little children
can't be choosy
(though I would
prefer to snooze
in my bed
if I could choose).
I will not
drive Mamma crazy,
I will not
at all be lazy,
I will jump
right out of bed
– and be Sleepy Lu
      instead.'

Scorching John
Harry Graham

John, who rode his Dunlop tyre
O'er the head of sweet Maryre,
When she died in frightful pain,
Had to blow it out again.

Nobody
Emily Dickinson

I'm Nobody! Who are you?
Are you – Nobody – too?
Then there's a pair of us!
Don't tell! they'd banish us – you know!

How dreary – to be – Somebody!
How public – like a Frog –
To tell your name – the livelong June –
To an admiring Bog!

Granny
Spike Milligan

Through every nook and every cranny
The wind blew in on poor old Granny;
Around her knees, into each ear
(And up her nose as well, I fear).

All through the night the wind grew worse,
It nearly made the vicar curse.
The top had fallen off the steeple
Just missing him (and other people).

It blew on man; it blew on beast.
It blew on nun; it blew on priest.
It blew the wig off Auntie Fanny –
But most of all, it blew on Granny!

Rhymes
Riddles
Logic
&
Folly

Milking

Anonymous

Two legs sat upon three legs,
With four legs standing by;
Four were then drawn by ten:
Read my riddle ye can't,
However much ye try.

A Cherry

Anonymous

As I went through the garden gap,
Who should I meet but Dick Red-cap!
A stick in his hand, a stone in his throat.
If you'll tell me this riddle, I'll give you a groat.

AEIOU
Jonathan Swift

We are very little creatures,
All of different voice and features;
One of us in glass is set,
One of us you'll find in jet.
T'other you may see in tin,
And the fourth a box within.
If the fifth you should pursue,
It can never fly from you.

Limericks

Edward Lear

There was an Old Man with a beard,
Who said, 'It is just as I feared! –
    Four Larks and a Wren,
    Two Owls and a Hen,
Have all built their nests in my beard!'

There was a Young Lady of Ryde,
Whose shoe-strings were seldom untied;
    She purchased some clogs
    And some small spotty dogs
And frequently walked about Ryde.

There was a Young Lady whose eyes
Were unique as to colour and size;
    When she opened them wide,
    People all turned aside,
And started away in surprise.

There was an Old Man of the Coast,
Who placidly sat on a post;
　　But when it was cold,
　　He relinquished his hold,
And called for some hot buttered toast.

There was an Old Man of the Dee,
Who was sadly annoyed by a flea;
　　When he said, 'I will scratch it' –
　　They gave him a hatchet,
Which grieved that Old Man of the Dee.

There was an Old Lady whose folly
Induced her to sit in a holly;
　　Whereupon by a thorn,
　　Her dress being torn,
She quickly became melancholy.

The Old Man of Blackheath
Anonymous

There was an old man of Blackheath
Who sat on his set of false teeth.
Said he, with a start,
'O, Lord, bless my heart!
I have bitten myself underneath!'

A Tree
Anonymous

In Spring I look gay,
Decked in comely array,
In Summer more clothing I wear;
When colder it grows
I fling off my clothes,
And in Winter quite naked appear.

Two Tongue Twisters

Carolyn Wells

A canner exceedingly canny
One morning remarked to his granny,
'A canner can can
Anything that he can,
But a canner can't can a can, can he?'

A tutor who tooted the flute
Tried to tutor two tooters to toot.
Said the two to the tutor,
'Is it harder to toot, or
To tutor two tooters to toot?'

Doctor Bell

Anonymous

Doctor Bell fell down the well
And broke his collar-bone.
Doctors should attend the sick
And leave the well alone.

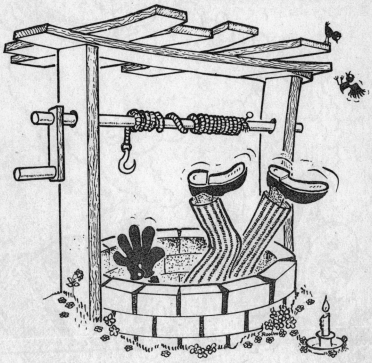

A Candle

Anonymous

Little Nancy Etticoat,
In a white petticoat,
And a red nose;
The longer she stands,
The shorter she grows.

Ask no questions

Michael Rosen

Ask no questions
tell no lies.
Ever seen mincemeat
in mince pies?

Career

Daniel Pettiward

I'd rather drive an engine than
Be a little gentleman;
I'd rather go shunting and hooting
Than hunting and shooting.

Frog
Anonymous

A froggie sat on a lily pad
Looking up at the sky:
The lily pad broke and the frog fell in,
Water all in his eye.

Rabbit
Anonymous

A rabbit raced a turtle,
You know the turtle won;
And Mister Bunny came in late,
A little hot cross bun!

Two Sad
William Cole

It's such a shock, I almost screech,
When I find a worm inside my peach!
But then, what *really* makes me blue
Is to find a worm who's bit in two!

Longing
Anonymous

I wish I was a little grub
With whiskers round my tummy
I'd climb into a honey-pot
And make my tummy gummy.

Vegetables

Shel Silverstein

Eat a tomato and you'll turn red
(I don't think that's really so);
Eat a carrot and you'll turn orange
(Still and all you never know);
Eat some spinach and you'll turn green
(I'm not saying that it's true
But that's what I heard, and so
I thought I'd pass it on to you).

Eating Habits

Anonymous

I eat my peas with honey,
I've done it all my life:
It makes the peas taste funny,
But it keeps them on the knife.

Mud

Polly Chase Boyden

Mud is very nice to feel
All squishy-squash between the toes!
I'd rather wade in wiggly mud
Than smell a yellow rose.
Nobody else but the rosebush knows
How nice mud feels
Between the toes.

Meetings and Absences 1
Roy Fuller

Nothing can really beat
For a quick sensuous treat
Clean socks on just-bathed feet.

Meetings and Absences 2
Roy Fuller

How does your little toe
In the bed so long and bare,
Keep on discovering
The top sheet's little tear?

Egg Thoughts
Russell Hoban

Soft Boiled
I do not like the way you slide,
I do not like your soft inside,
I do not like you many ways,
And I could do for many days
Without a soft-boiled egg.

Sunny-Side-Up
With their yolks and whites all runny
They are looking at me funny.

Sunny-Side-Down
Lying face-down on the plate
On their stomachs there they wait.

Poached
Poached eggs on toast, why do you shiver
With such a funny little quiver?

Scrambled
I eat as well as I am able,
But some falls underneath the table.

Hard-Boiled
With so much suffering today
Why do them any other way?

The Poultries

Ogden Nash

Let's think of eggs.
They have no legs.
Chickens come from eggs
But they have legs.
The plot thickens;
Eggs come from chickens,
But have no legs under 'em.
What a conundrum!

The Rain
Baron Charles Bowen

The rain it raineth on the just
And also on the unjust fella.
But chiefly on the just, because
The unjust steals the just's umbrella.

Rain
Spike Milligan

There are holes in the sky
Where the rain gets in,
But they're ever so small
That's why rain is thin.

Treks & Travels

The Duck and the Kangaroo

Edward Lear

Said the Duck to the Kangaroo,
'Good gracious! how you hop!
Over the fields and the water too,
As if you never would stop!
My life is a bore in this nasty pond,
And I long to go out in the world beyond!
I wish I could hop like you!'
Said the Duck to the Kangaroo.

'Please give me a ride on your back!'
Said the Duck to the Kangaroo.
'I would sit quite still, and say nothing but "Quack",
The whole of the long day through!
And we'd go to the Dee, and the Jelly Bo Lee,
Over the land, and over the sea;
Please take me a ride! O do!'
Said the Duck to the Kangaroo.

Said the Kangaroo to the Duck,
'This requires some little reflection;
Perhaps on the whole it might bring me luck,
And there seems but one objection,
Which is, if you'll let me speak so bold,
Your feet are unpleasantly wet and cold,
And would probably give me the roo-
Matiz!' said the Kangaroo.

Said the Duck, 'As I sat on the rocks,
I have thought over that completely,
And I bought four pairs of worsted socks
Which fit my web-feet neatly.
And to keep out the cold I've bought a cloak,
And every day a cigar I'll smoke,
All to follow my own dear true
Love of a Kangaroo!'

Said the Kangaroo, 'I'm ready!
All in the moonlight pale;
But to balance me well, dear Duck, sit steady!
And quite at the end of my tail!'
So away they went with a hop and a bound,
And they hopped the whole world three times round;
And who so happy, – O who,
As the Duck and the Kangaroo?

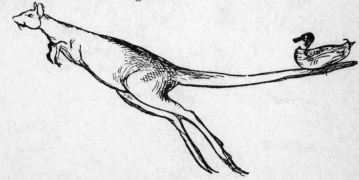

If Pigs Could Fly
James Reeves

If pigs could fly, I'd fly a pig
To foreign countries small and big –
To Italy and Spain,
To Austria, where cowbells ring,
To Germany, where people sing –
And then come home again.

I'd see the Ganges and the Nile;
I'd visit Madagascar's isle,
And Persia and Peru.
People would say they'd never seen
So odd, so strange an air-machine
As that on which I flew.

Why, everyone would raise a shout
To see his trotters and his snout
Come floating from the sky;
And I would be a famous star
Well known in countries near and far –
If only pigs could fly!

Buckingham Palace

A. A. Milne

They're changing guard at Buckingham Palace –
Christopher Robin went down with Alice.
Alice is marrying one of the guard.
'A soldier's life is terrible hard,'
            Says Alice.

They're changing guard at Buckingham Palace –
Christopher Robin went down with Alice.
We saw a guard in a sentry-box.
'One of the sergeants looks after their socks,'
            Says Alice.

They're changing guard at Buckingham Palace –
Christopher Robin went down with Alice.
We looked for the King, but he never came.
'Well, God take care of him, all the same,'
            Says Alice.

They're changing guard at Buckingham Palace –
Christopher Robin went down with Alice.
They've great big parties inside the grounds.
'I wouldn't be King for a hundred pounds,'
            Says Alice.

They're changing guard at Buckingham Palace –
Christopher Robin went down with Alice.
A face looked out, but it wasn't the King's.
'He's much too busy a-signing things,'
            Says Alice.

They're changing guard at Buckingham Palace –
Christopher Robin went down with Alice.
'Do you think the King knows all about *me*?'
'Sure to, dear, but it's time for tea,'
            Says Alice.

I Visit The Queen
Gregory Harrison

Ferdinand, Ferdinand,
Where have you been?
I've been up to London to look at the queen.
I've been with two horses,
A black and a grey;
They ate fifteen bundles
Of sweet-smelling hay.
At Buckingham Palace I stopped at the gate
And explained to the sentry why I was late.
The railings were splendid in black and in gold
And I tied up the horses and walked in the cold
Across the wide courtyard; the steps were so broad,
And someone in frockcoat, said 'Ticket, my Lord?'
I felt in my pocket – I knew it was there –
Mixed up with dog biscuits, an apple and pear.
And I bowed to the queen, and would you believe,
I remembered to cover the hole in my sleeve.
The queen very graciously chose not to see
The string round my trousers, the tear at my knee.
Ferdinand, Ferdinand,
Where have you been?
I've been up to London to look at the queen.
Ferdinand, Ferdinand,
What did you there?
I knelt to the queen and she touched my grey hair.

Mr Pennycomequick

Charles Causley

Mr Hector Pennycomequick
Stood on the castle keep,
Opened up a carriage-umbrella
And took a mighty leap.

'Hooray!' cried Mr Pennycomequick
As he went through the air.
'I've always wanted to go like this
From here to Newport Square.'

But Mr Hector Pennycomequick
He never did float nor fly.
He landed in an ivy-bush,
His legs up in the sky.

Mr Hector Pennycomequick
They hurried home to bed
With a bump the size of a sea-gull's egg
On the top of his head.

'So sorry,' said Mr Pennycomequick,
'For causing all this fuss.
When next I go to Newport Square
I think I'll take the bus.'

The moral of this little tale
Is difficult to refute:
A carriage-umbrella's a carriage-umbrella
And not a parachute.

Mr Skinner

N. M. Bodecker

Orville Skinner
(kite-string spinner)
never stopped
to eat his dinner,
for he found it
too exciting
and rewarding
to go kiting.
Flying kites,
he used to sing:
'I'm a spinner
on a string!'
When they warned him:
'Mister Skinner,
capable
but high-strung spinner,
it may take you
to Brazil,'
Skinner cried:
'I hope it will!'

Australian Visitor
Gregory Harrison

I went to London recently
And took a 9a bus,
And found that I was seated by
A duck-billed platypus.

Of course, there's nothing odd or strange
About this slight event,
But I admit I was intrigued
To see which way he went.

He held a sticky ten-pence coin
Flat on his skin-webbed hand,
And with antipodean voice
Asked clearly for the Strand.

I knew then by his accent,
I knew and I was right,
He'd get off at Australia House
And sleep there for the night.

I said to him, 'Nice evening;'
He turned his flattened jaws;
He made as if to answer me
And offered me his paws.

A double-handed handshake,
I thought, is rather grand;
He just had time to say, 'Indeed,'
When someone shouted, 'Strand.'

It's hard to get off quickly
When your legs are rather short,
And I had a sudden panic
When his poison spur got caught.

It was tucked inside my pocket –
Could it really kill a man?
But he freed it with his five strong nails
And shuffled down and ran.

He ran along the centre aisle
And stepped into the street;
A cycle following behind
Just missed his little feet.

'Goodbye,' I shouted, 'and Good Luck.'
I wish there had been time
To talk of Platypus affairs
In Platypussian mime.

Passengers stared through windows
And made a dreadful fuss,
And all because they'd travelled with
A duck-billed platypus.

They gazed at me and whispered,
'I'm sure. Whatever next!'
Until their silly chattering
Stirred me till I was vexed.

The driver gaped with open mouth,
Then turned to look at me;
'I say. That something from a zoo
That's just got blinking free?'

I rose with dignity and said,
'You all are most unkind.
That was a most distinguished – er – man
That you have left behind.

'Of course he's rather primitive,
His family's very old;
How rude to stare and spy upon
A stranger in the cold.

'Are you "Monotremata"?'
They shrank before my frown.
'No, I suppose your family tree
Is Smith or Jones or Brown.'

The bus had stopped, they turned and looked,
Their eyes were opened wide;
Outside Australia House he bowed
And disappeared inside.

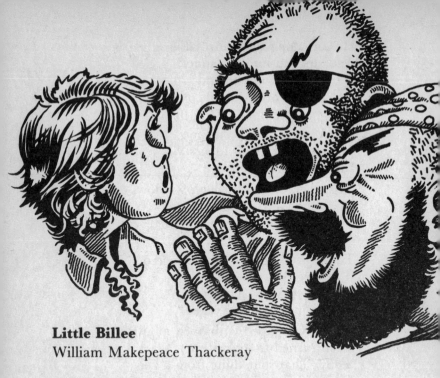

Little Billee
William Makepeace Thackeray

There were three sailors of Bristol city
Who took a boat and went to sea.
But first with beef and captain's biscuits
And pickled pork they loaded she.

There was gorging Jack and guzzling Jimmy,
And the youngest he was little Billee.
Now when they got as far as the Equator
They'd nothing left but one split pea.

Says gorging Jack to guzzling Jimmy,
'I am extremely hungaree.'
To gorging Jack says guzzling Jimmy,
'We've nothing left, us must eat we.'

Says gorging Jack to guzzling Jimmy,
'With one another we shouldn't agree!
There's little Bill, he's young and tender,
We're old and tough so let's eat he.'

94

'Oh! Billy, we're going to kill and eat you
So undo the button of your chemie.'
When Bill received this information
He used his pocket handkerchie.

'First let me say my catechism,
Which my poor mammy taught to me.'
'Make haste, make haste,' says guzzling Jimmy,
While Jack pulled out his snickersnee.

So Billy went up to the main-topgallant mast,
And down he fell on his bended knee.
He scarce had come to the twelfth commandment
When up he jumps. 'There's land I see:

'Jerusalem and Madagascar,
And North and South Amerikee:
There's the British flag a-riding at anchor,
With Admiral Napier, K.C.B.'

So when they got aboard of the Admiral's,
He hanged fat Jack and flogged Jimmee;
But as for little Bill he made him
The Captain of a Seventy-three.

Joshua Lane
Anonymous

'I know I have lost my train,'
Said a man named Joshua Lane;
'But I'll run on the rails
With my coat-tails for sails
And maybe I'll catch it again.'

The Nutcrackers and the Sugar-Tongs

Edward Lear

The Nutcrackers sate by a plate on the table,
The Sugar-tongs sate by a plate at his side;
And the Nutcrackers said, 'Don't you wish we were able
'Along the blue hills and green meadows to ride?
'Must we drag on this stupid existence for ever,
'So idle and weary, so full of remorse, –
'While every one else takes his pleasure, and never
'Seems happy unless he is riding a horse?

'Don't you think we could ride without being instructed?
'Without any saddle, or bridle, or spur?
'Our legs are so long, and so aptly constructed,
'I'm sure that an accident could not occur.
'Let us all of a sudden hop down from the table,
'And hustle downstairs, and each jump on a horse!
'Shall we try? Shall we go? Do you think we are able?'
The Sugar-tongs answered distinctly, 'Of course!'

So down the long staircase they hopped in a minute,
The Sugar-tongs snapped, and Crackers said 'crack!'
The stable was open, the horses were in it;
Each took out a pony, and jumped on his back.
The Cat in a fright scrambled out of the doorway,
The Mice tumbled out of a bundle of hay,
The brown and white Rats, and the black ones from Norwa
Screamed out, 'They are taking the horses away!'

The whole of the household was filled with amazement,
The Cups and the Saucers danced madly about,
The Plates and the Dishes looked out of the casement,
The Saltcellar stood on his head with a shout,
The Spoons with a clatter looked out of the lattice,
The Mustard-pot climbed up the Gooseberry Pies,
The Soup-ladle peeped through a heap of Veal Patties,
And squeaked with a ladle-like scream of surprise.

The Frying-pan said, 'It's an awful delusion!'
The Tea-kettle hissed and grew black in the face;
And they all rushed downstairs in the wildest confusion,
To see the great Nutcracker-Sugar-tong race.
And out of the stable, with screamings and laughter,
(Their ponies were cream-coloured, speckled with brown,)
The Nutcrackers first, and the Sugar-tongs after,
Rode all round the yard, and then all round the town.

They rode through the street, and they rode by the station,
They galloped away to the beautiful shore;
In silence they rode, and 'made no observation',
Save this: 'We will never go back any more!'
And still you might hear, till they rode out of hearing,
The Sugar-tongs snap, and the Crackers say 'crack!'
Till far in the distance their forms disappearing,
They faded away. – And they never came back!

I started Early
Emily Dickinson

I started Early – Took my Dog –
And visited the Sea –
The Mermaids in the Basement
Came out to look at me –

And Frigates – in the Upper Floor
Extended Hempen Hands –
Presuming Me to be a Mouse –
Aground – upon the Sands –

But no Man moved Me – till the Tide
Went past my simple Shoe –
And past my Apron – and my Belt
And past my Boddice – too –

And made as He would eat me up –
As wholly as a Dew
Upon a Dandelion's Sleeve –
And then – I started – too –

And He – He followed – close behind –
I felt His Silver Heel
Upon my Ancle – Then my Shoes
Would overflow with Pearl –

Until We met the Solid Town –
No One He seemed to know –
And bowing – with a Mighty look –
At me – The Sea withdrew –

The Lost Shoe
Walter de la Mare

Poor little Lucy
By some mischance,
Lost her shoe
As she did dance:
'Twas not on the stairs,
Not in the hall;
Not where they sat
At supper at all.
She looked in the garden,
But there it was not;
Henhouse, or kennel,
Or high dovecote.
Dairy and meadow,
And wild woods through
Showed not a trace
Of Lucy's shoe.
Bird nor bunny
Nor glimmering moon
Breathed a whisper
Of where 'twas gone.
It was cried and cried,
Oyez and Oyez!
In French, Dutch, Latin,
And Portuguese.
Ships the dark seas
Went plunging through,
But none brought news
Of Lucy's shoe;
And still she patters
In silk and leather,
O'er snow, sand, shingle,
In every weather;
Spain, and Africa,
Hindustan,
Java, China,
And lamped Japan;
Plain and desert,
She hops – hops through,
Pernambuco
To gold Peru;
Mountain and forest,
And river too,
All the world over
For her lost shoe.

The Jumblies

Edward Lear

They went to sea in a Sieve, they did,
In a Sieve they went to sea:
In spite of all their friends could say,
On a winter's morn, on a stormy day,
In a Sieve they went to sea!
And when the Sieve turned round and round,
And every one cried, 'You'll all be drowned!'
They called aloud, 'Our Sieve ain't big,
But we don't care a button! we don't care a fig!
In a Sieve we'll go to sea!'
Far and few, far and few,
Are the lands where the Jumblies live;
Their heads are green, and their hands are blue,
And they went to sea in a Sieve.

They sailed away in a Sieve, they did,
In a Sieve they sailed so fast,
With only a beautiful pea-green veil
Tied with a riband by way of a sail,
To a small tobacco-pipe mast;
And every one said, who saw them go,
'Oh won't they be soon upset, you know!
For the sky is dark, and the voyage is long,
And happen what may, it's extremely wrong
In a Sieve to sail so fast!'
Far and few, far and few,
Are the lands where the Jumblies live;
Their heads are green, and their hands are blue,
And they went to sea in a Sieve.

The water it soon came in, it did,
The water it soon came in;
So to keep them dry, they wrapped their feet
In a pinky paper all folded neat,
And they fastened it down with a pin.
And they passed the night in a crockery-jar,
And each of them said, 'How wise we are!
Though the sky be dark, and the voyage be long,
Yet we never can think we were rash or wrong,
While round in our Sieve we spin!'
Far and few, far and few,
Are the lands where the Jumblies live;
Their heads are green, and their hands are blue,
And they went to sea in a Sieve.

And all night long they sailed away;
And when the sun went down,
They whistled and warbled a moony song
To the echoing sound of a coppery gong,
In the shade of the mountains brown.
'O Timballo! How happy we are,
When we live in a sieve and a crockery-jar,
And all night long in the moonlight pale,
We sail away with a pea-green sail,
In the shade of the mountains brown!'
Far and few, far and few,
Are the lands where the Jumblies live;
Their heads are green, and their hands are blue,
And they went to sea in a Sieve.

They sailed to the Western Sea, they did,
To a land all covered with trees,
And they bought an Owl, and a useful Cart,
And a pound of Rice, and a Cranberry Tart,
And a hive of silvery Bees.

And they bought a Pig, and some green Jack-daws,
And a lovely Monkey with lollipop paws,
And forty bottles of Ring-Bo-Ree,
And no end of Stilton Cheese.
Far and few, far and few,
Are the lands where the Jumblies live;
Their heads are green, and their hands are blue,
And they went to sea in a Sieve.

And in twenty years they all came back
In twenty years or more,
And every one said, 'How tall they've grown!
For they've been to the Lakes, and the Torrible Zone,
And the hills of the Chankly Bore';
And they drank their health, and gave them a feast
Of dumplings made of beautiful yeast;
And every one said, 'If we only live,
We too will go to sea in a Sieve, –
To the hills of the Chankly Bore!'
Far and few, far and few,
Are the lands where the Jumblies live;
Their heads are green, and their hands are blue,
And they went to sea in a Sieve.

Adventures & Mishaps

Franklin Hyde

*Who caroused in the Dirt and was corrected by His
Uncle.*

Hilaire Belloc

His Uncle came on Franklin Hyde
Carousing in the Dirt.
He Shook him hard from Side to Side
And
Hit him till it Hurt,
Exclaiming, with a Final Thud,
'Take that! Abandoned Boy!
For Playing with Disgusting Mud
As though it were a Toy!'

MORAL

From Franklin Hyde's adventure, learn
To pass your Leisure Time
In Cleanly Merriment, and turn
From Mud and Ooze and Slime
And every form of Nastiness –
But, on the other Hand,
Children in ordinary Dress
May always play with Sand.

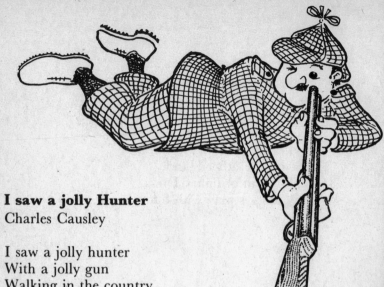

I saw a jolly Hunter
Charles Causley

I saw a jolly hunter
With a jolly gun
Walking in the country
In the jolly sun.

In the jolly meadow
Sat a jolly hare.
Saw the jolly hunter.
Took jolly care.

Hunter jolly eager –
Sight of jolly prey.
Forgot gun pointing
Wrong jolly way.

Jolly hunter jolly head
Over heels gone.
Jolly old safety-catch
Not jolly on.

Bang went the jolly gun.
Hunter jolly dead.
Jolly hare got clean away.
Jolly good, I said.

The Termite
Ogden Nash

Some primal termite knocked on wood
And tasted it, and found it good;
And that is why your Cousin May
Fell through the parlour floor today.

The Generals

Shel Silverstein

Said General Clay to General Gore.
'Oh *must* we fight this silly war,
To kill and die is such a bore.'
'I quite agree,' said General Gore.

Said General Gore to General Clay,
'We *could* go to the beach today
And have some ice cream on the way.'
'A *grand* idea,' said General Clay.

Said General Clay to General Gore,
'We'll build sand castles on the shore.'
Said General Gore, 'We'll splash and play.'
'Let's go *right now*,' said General Clay.

Said General Gore to General Clay,
'But what if the sea is *closed* today?
And what if the sand's been blown away?'
'A *dreadful* thought,' said General Clay.

Said General Gore to General Clay,
'I've always feared the ocean's spray
And we may drown – it's true, we may,
And we may even drown today.'
'Too true, too true,' said General Clay.

Said General Clay to General Gore,
'My bathing suit is slightly tore,
We'd better go on with our war.'
'I quite agree,' said General Gore.

Then General Clay charged General Gore
As bullets flew and cannon roared.
And now, alas! there is no more
Of General Clay and General Gore.

Hallelujah!

A. E. Housman

'Hallelujah!' was the only observation
That escaped Lieutenant-Colonel Mary Jane,
When she tumbled off the platform in the station,
And was cut in little pieces by the train.
    Mary Jane, the train is through yer!
    Hallelujah, Hallelujah!
We shall gather up the fragments that remain.

Disobedience

A. A. Milne

James James
Morrison Morrison
Weatherby George Dupree
Took great
Care of his Mother,
Though he was only three.
James James
Said to his Mother,
'Mother,' he said, said he;
'You must never go down to the end of the town, if
                      you don't go down with me.'

James James
Morrison's Mother
Put on a golden gown,
James James
Morrison's Mother
Drove to the end of the town.
James James
Morrison's Mother
Said to herself, said she:
'I can get right down to the end of the town and be
                      back in time for tea.'

King John
Put up a notice,
'LOST or STOLEN or STRAYED!
JAMES JAMES
MORRISON'S MOTHER
SEEMS TO HAVE BEEN MISLAID.
LAST SEEN
WANDERING VAGUELY:
QUITE OF HER OWN ACCORD,
SHE TRIED TO GET DOWN TO THE END OF
THE TOWN – *FORTY SHILLINGS REWARD*!

James James
Morrison Morrison
(Commonly known as Jim)
Told his
Other relations
Not to go blaming *him*.
James James
Said to his Mother,
'Mother,' he said, said he:
'You must *never* go down to the end of the town without
consulting me.'

James James
Morrison's mother
Hasn't been heard of since.
King John
Said he was sorry,
So did the Queen and Prince.
King John
(Somebody told me)
Said to a man he knew:
'If people go down to the end of the town, well what can
anyone do?'

(*Now then, very softly*)

J.J.
M.M.
W.G. Du P.
Took great
C/o his M*****
Though he was only 3.
J.J.
Said to his M*****
'M*****,' he said, said he:
'You-must-never-go-down-to-the-end-of-the-town-if-
you-don't-go-down-with-ME!'

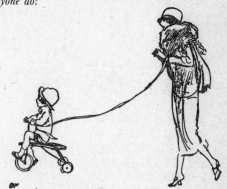

Picnic

Hugh Lofting

Ella, fell a
Maple tree.
Hilda, build a
Fire for me.

Teresa, squeeze a
Lemon, so.
Amanda, hand a
Plate to Flo.

Nora, pour a
Cup of tea.
Fancy, Nancy,
What a spree!

Henry King

Hilaire Belloc

The Chief Defect of Henry King
Was chewing little bits of String.
At last he swallowed some which tied
Itself in ugly Knots inside.

Physicians of the Utmost Fame
Were called at once; but when they came
They answered, as they took their Fees,
'There is no Cure for this Disease.

'Henry will very soon be dead.'
His Parents stood about his Bed
Lamenting his Untimely Death,
When Henry, with his Latest Breath,

Cried, 'Oh, my Friends, be warned by me,
That Breakfast, Dinner, Lunch, and Tea,
Are all the Human Frame requires ...'
With that, the Wretched Child expires.

Helicopter

Gregory Harrison

Heli, Heli, Heli,
Copter,
Miss Brown was strolling when it stopped her;
Very, very nearly dropped her
Shopping-bag in sudden fright
At the monstrous clatter-flight.
All the men lean on their spades
And watch the flashing rotor-blades.
Gavin (watching television plays)
Yelled, 'Look, a coastal rescue chopper –
Most exciting thing for days –
Isn't it a yellow whopper?'
Like a maddened bumble-bee
It has him twisting round to see;
Makes all the village heads corkscrew
To wave a welcome to the crew,
Who nonchalant through open door
Wave as they squat upon the floor.
Gavin (and all the racing boys)
Rejoices in the noose of noise;
But stern Miss Brown now flushed with rage
Is scribbling a double page.
'Write to the paper, yes, I must;
I shall express my deep disgust.'
While in a near-by field the sheep,
A woolly, lumpy, startled heap,
Bolted,
Halted,
Cropped a
Little fainter,
Bewildered by the helicopter.

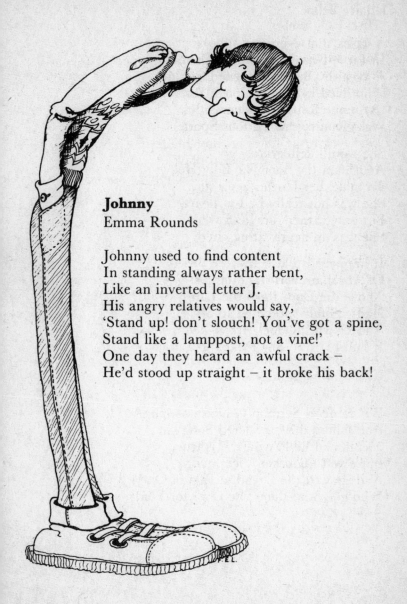

Johnny
Emma Rounds

Johnny used to find content
In standing always rather bent,
Like an inverted letter J.
His angry relatives would say,
'Stand up! don't slouch! You've got a spine,
Stand like a lamppost, not a vine!'
One day they heard an awful crack –
He'd stood up straight – it broke his back!

Rebecca

Who slammed Doors for Fun and Perished Miserably

Hilaire Belloc

A Trick that everyone abhors
In Little Girls is slamming Doors.
A Wealthy Banker's Little Daughter
Who lived in Palace Green, Bayswater
(By name Rebecca Offendort),
Was given to this Furious Sport.

She would deliberately go
And Slam the door like Billy-Ho!
To make her Uncle Jacob start.
She was not really bad at heart,
But only rather rude and wild;
She was an aggravating child.

It happened that a Marble Bust
Of Abraham was standing just
Above the Door this little Lamb
Had carefully prepared to Slam,
And Down it came! It knocked her flat!
It laid her out! She looked like that!

* * * * * * * *

Her Funeral Sermon (which was long
And followed by a Sacred Song)
Mentioned her Virtues, it is true,
But dwelt upon her Vices, too,
And showed the Dreadful End of One
Who goes and slams the Door for Fun.

Bad Dog

Brian Lee

All day long, Bones hasn't been seen
– But now he comes slinking home
Smelling of ditches and streams
And pastures and pinewoods and loam
And tries to crawl under my bed.
His coat is caked with mud,
And one of his ears drips blood.
Nobody knows where he's been.

'Who did it?' they ask him, 'who ...?
He'll have to be bathed ... the sinner ...
Pack him off to his basket ...
You *bad dog*, you'll get no dinner ...'
And he cowers, and rolls an eye.
Tomorrow, I *won't* let him go –
But he licks my hand, and then – oh,
How I wish that I had been too.

The Story of Fidgety Philip
Heinrich Hoffman

One evening Philip's father said,
'You twist and squirm and shake your head.
Come, let us see if you are able
To sit quite still for once at table.'
But not a word
Had Philip heard.
He giggled
And wiggled
And wriggled
And tottered
And teetered
And rocked in his chair.
Till his father cried, 'Philip!
Sit still – or beware!'

Caring nothing for disaster,
Backwards, forwards, always faster,
Philip rocked – until the chair
Slipped from under. Then and there
Philip grabbed the table cloth,
Spilling everything: the broth,
Bread and butter, all the dishes,
Goblets, gravy, meat and fishes,
Cauliflower, garden greens,
Spinach, parsnips, peas and beans,
Pastry, puddings white and brown ...
Everything came tumbling down!

Meanwhile where was Philip? There,
Underneath the ruined chair,
Underneath – as you might guess –
Broken plates, a horrid mess,
Groaning in a hideous mood,
Soaked from head to toe with food.
And, to make his plight complete,
Nothing left for him to eat!

Willie Built a Guillotine

William E. Engel

Willie built a guillotine,
Tried it out on sister Jean.
Said Mother as she got the mop:
'These messy games have got to stop!'

The Old Man of Torbay
'A Nobody'

There was an old man of Torbay
Who said to his wife one day
At twelve of the clock, prepare for a shock
For I shall be floating away.

That venturesome man of Torbay
Was put in a barrel that day
They corked it up tight, and it floated upright
Far out to sea from the bay.

That nautical man of Torbay
Wobbled and rolled all the way
To a strange foreign land all coral and sand
Where turtles and penguins do play.

Of that bumptious old man of Torbay
A tale shall be written one day
For a cannibal slim, did promptly cook him
And pickled that man of Torbay.

Doctor Foster

Anonymous

Doctor Foster went to Gloucester
In a shower of rain;
He stepped in a puddle,
Right up to his middle,
And never went there again.

George

Who played with a Dangerous Toy, and suffered a
Catastrophe of considerable Dimensions
Hilaire Belloc

When George's Grandmamma was told
That George had been as good as Gold,
She Promised in the Afternoon
To buy him an *Immense* BALLOON.

And so she did; but when it came,
It got into the candle flame,
And being of a dangerous sort
Exploded with a loud report!

The Lights went out! The Windows broke!
The Room was filled with reeking smoke.
And in the darkness shrieks and yells
Were mingled with Electric Bells,
And falling masonry and groans,
And crunching, as of broken bones,
And dreadful shrieks, when, worst of all,
The House itself began to fall!
It tottered, shuddering to and fro,
Then crashed into the street below –
Which happened to be Savile Row.

* * * * * * * *

When Help arrived, among the Dead
Were Cousin Mary, Little Fred,
The Footmen (both of them), The Groom,
The man that cleaned the Billiard-Room,
The Chaplain, and the Still-Room Maid.
And I am dreadfully afraid
That Monsieur Champignon, the Chef,
Will now be permanently deaf –
And both his Aides much the same;
While George, who was in part to blame,
Received, you will regret to hear,
A nasty lump behind the ear.

MORAL

The moral is that little Boys
Should not be given dangerous Toys.

Mary Pugh

Spike Milligan

Mary Pugh
Was nearly two
When she went out of doors.
She went out standing up she did
But came back on all fours.
The moral of the story
Please meditate and pause:
Never send a baby out
With loosely waisted draws.

Caspar and the Soup

Heinrich Hoffman

Caspar was never sick at all;
His body was a butter-ball;
Solid he was from head to feet;
His cheeks were red. He loved to eat.
Yet suddenly one dismal day
His parents heard young Caspar say:
'I don't want soup. Take it away!
No soup!' he screamed. 'Take it away!
No matter what! No matter when!
I'll never drink a drop again!'

Next day he would not touch his dinner
And – as you see – he grew much thinner.
But still he cried, 'I beg and pray,
Remove the stuff! Take it away!
I will not eat my soup today!'

Then, on the third day of the week
Caspar began to pale and peak.
But, as the soup came to the table,
He screamed as loud as he was able:
'Remove the plate! Take it away!
I will not eat my soup today!
I will *not* eat my soup today!'

When four more soupless days had passed
Caspar was skin and bones at last.
He was no thicker than a thread.
And on the fifth day he was dead.
Burying the boy they could not save,
They put a soup-plate on his grave.

The Death of a Mad Dog

Oliver Goldsmith

Good people all, of every sort,
Give ear unto my song;
And if you find it wondrous short, –
It cannot hold you long.

In Islington there was a man,
Of whom the world might say
That still a godly race he ran, –
Whene'er he went to pray.

A kind and gentle heart he had,
To comfort friends and foes;
The naked every day he clad, –
When he put on his clothes.

And in that town a dog was found,
As many dogs there be,
Both mongrel, puppy, whelp, and hound,
And curs of low degree.

The dog and man at first were friends;
But when a pique began,
The dog, to gain some private ends,
Went mad, and bit the man.

Around from all the neighbouring streets,
The wondering neighbours ran,
And swore the dog had lost his wits
To bite so good a man.

The wound it seemed both sore and sad
To every Christian eye;
And while they swore the dog was mad,
They swore the man would die.

But soon a wonder came to light,
That showed the rogues they lied;
The man recovered from the bite,
The dog it was that died.

The Sad Story of a Little Boy that Cried
Anonymous

Once a little boy, Jack, was oh! ever so good,
Till he took a strange notion to cry all he could.

So he cried all the day, and he cried all the night,
He cried in the morning and in the twilight;

He cried till his voice was as hoarse as a crow,
And his mouth grew so large it looked like a great O.
It grew at the bottom, and grew at the top;
It grew till they thought that it never would stop.

Each day his great mouth grew taller and taller,
And his dear little self grew smaller and smaller.

At last, that same mouth grew so big that – alack! –
It was only a mouth with a border of Jack.

Acknowledgments

The publishers wish to thank the following for their kind permission to use their material:
The Bison, The Elephant, The Polar Bear, The Vulture, Franklin Hyde, Henry King, Rebecca, George:
Hilaire Belloc, Gerald Duckworth & Co. Ltd. *Howard* from 'The Sunny Side' and *Disobedience*
from 'When We Were Very Young': A. A. Milne, and *Yak*: 1956/7 William Jay Smith,
Curtis Brown Ltd. *Jump or Jiggle*: Evelyn Beyer from 'Another Here and Now Story Book':
Lucy Sprague Mitchell © 1937 by E. P. Dutton; renewal copyright © 1965 by Lucy Sprague
Mitchell, reprinted by permission of the publisher, E. P. Dutton. *Silly Old Baboon* from 'A Book of
Milliganimals', *Rain* from 'A Dustbin of Milligan', *Go North, South, East and West, Young Man* from 'A
Book of Bits or a Bit of a Book', *To-day I saw a little worm, I'm not frightened of Pussy Cats, Granny,
Mary Pugh* from 'Silly Verse for Kids': Spike Milligan, Dobson Books Ltd. *The Angry Hens from
Never-When* and *Ask no Questions* from 'Wouldn't You Like to Know': Michael Rosen, *Stables' Tables*
from 'Seen Grandpa Lately?' and *Meetings and Absences* from 'Poor Roy': Roy Fuller, André
Deutsch Ltd. *The Octopus, The Firefly, The Termite*: the Estate of the late Ogden Nash. *The
Old Gumbie Cat* from 'Old Possum's Book of Practical Cats': T. S. Eliot, *The Geese in Greece,
Lazy Lucy, Mr Skinner* from 'Let's Marry said the Cherry': N. M. Bodecker, *Among the
Mountains of Spitzbergen, My Sister Clarissa* from 'To Aylsham Fair': George Barker, *The Whale*
from 'The Collected Poems of Theodore Roethke', *My Uncle Dan* from 'Meet my Folks': Ted
Hughes, and *Bees* and *Egg Thoughts* from 'Egg Thoughts and Other Frances Songs': Russell
Hoban, Faber and Faber Ltd. *The Kwackagee* from 'More Prefabulous Animiles': James
Reeves, William Heinemann Ltd. *One Day at the Perranporth Pet Shop, King Foo Foo*, and *Mr
Pennycomequick* from 'Figgie Hobbin', and *I Saw A Jolly Hunter* from 'Collected Poems':
Charles Causley, Macmillan & Co. Ltd. *Piano Practice*: © Ian Serraillier 1963. *The Yellow
Cat, Miss Torrent, A Fat Old Farmer, I Visit the Queen, Australian Visitor*, and *Helicopter* from
'The Night of the Wild Horses': Gregory Harrison (1971), *If Pigs Could Fly* from 'The
Blackbird in the Lilac': James Reeves (1952), Oxford University Press. *Armadillo* from 'A
Book of Creatures': Mary Innes and *How Sad* from 'A Boy Named Mary Jane': William
Cole, Franklin Watts Limited. *Old Mr Bows*: Wilma Horsbrugh. *Pigs* from 'The Queen of
Eene': Jack Prelutsky Text Copyright © 1970, 1978 by Jack Prelutsky, by permission of
Greenwillow Books (a division of William Morrow & Company). *Buckingham Palace* from
'When We Were Very Young': A. A. Milne, Methuen Children's Books Ltd. *Mister Beers* and
Picnic from 'Porridge Poetry': Hugh Lofting, Christopher Lofting, Jonathan Cape Ltd.
Nobody and *I Started Early* reprinted by permission of the publishers and the Trustees of
Amherst College from 'The Poems of Emily Dickinson, edited by Thomas H. Johnson,
Cambridge, Mass.: The Belknap Press of Harvard University Press, Copyright © 1951, 1955
by the President and Fellows of Harvard College. *Uncle, Politeness, Inconsiderate Hannah*, and
Scorching John from 'Most Ruthless Rhymes for Heartless Homes': Harry Graham, Edward
Arnold (Publishers) Ltd. *Kings, The Lost Shoe*: The Literary Trustees of Walter de la Mare
and The Society of Authors as their representative. *Hallelujah*: The Society of Authors as the
literary representative of the Estate A. E. Housman; and Jonathan Cape Ltd., publishers of
A. E. Housman's 'Collected Poems'. *Career*: Daniel Pettiward by permission of *Punch*. *Bad Dog*
and *Our Bonfire* from 'Late Home': © 1976 Brian Lee, Kestrel Books, a division of Penguin
Books Ltd., 1976, reprinted by permission of Penguin Books Ltd. *Johnny*: Emma Rounds
from 'Creative Youth': Hughes Mearns © 1925 by Doubleday & Company Inc. *The Generals* from
'Where the Sidewalk Ends' by Shel Silverstein. Copyright © 1974 by Shel Silverstein. By
permission of Harper & Row, Publishers, Inc. *Vegetables* by Shel Silverstein. Copyright © 1972. By
permission of William Cole. Whilst every reasonable effort has been made to find the copyright
owners of the works in this book the publishers apologize to any that they have been unable to
trace and will insert an acknowledgment in future editions upon notification of the fact.